WELCOME

SOME HOME COOKING RECIPES

Making homemade dog food means you won't have to worry about additives and preservatives, which are present in store-bought food and are harmful to your dog's health. Just like you... a freshly made home-cooked meal tastes so much better.

If you're planning to cook Frenchie recipes from our cookbook, you should consult your vet first. Dog breeds differ greatly in terms of their nutritional requirements. Furthermore, French Bulldogs are more likely to have obesity and food allergies. The big, sad eyes are hard to resist, but their health is more important.

It is also important for your Frenchie to make this transition slowly when introducing new foods or a new diet. To prevent stomach upset, you can give half the new food and half of their old food simultaneously.

For those who love Frenchies, the Frenchie Cookbook offers a collection of recipes, tips, and advice. This cookbook took a lot of work to put together, including many hours spent cooking, testing, and writing all the recipes. The cookbook and accompanying materials were prepared with the utmost care by the authors. Concerning accuracy, appropriateness, fitness, or completeness, the author doesn't makes any representations or warranties.

FRENCHIE COOKBOOK

CONTENTS

Welcome	2
Contents	3
Frenchie Weekly Meals	4 - 19
Sensitive Stomach Frenchie Recipes	20 - 31
For the Dieting French Bulldog.	32 - 43
Special Occasions	44 - 53
French Bulldog Treats	54 - 79

Frenchie Weekly Meals

Frenchie Weekly Meals

Now you can ditch the store-bought dog food that is often loaded with unnecessary ingredients and preservatives. Your Frenchie will wuv you even more with these healthy weekly recipes. They are easy and cost-efficient and are freezer friendly.

French Bulldog Chicken Soup

RELATIVELY EASY   **SLOW COOKER**   **COOKED FOOD DIET**

Ingredients

- 3 pieces unseasoned chicken
- 3 carrots
- 1 stalk of celery
- 1 sweet potato
- 1 handful of raw green beans
- 1 tsp of chicken base
- Water

Directions

1. Add chicken pieces to a pot, cover with water and add the tsp of chicken base. Cook for approximately one hour or untill chicken is tender and cooked.

2. Slice up vegetables and put the vegetables in a pot, covering it with water.

3. On medium heat, cook the veggies for approximately one hour or untill soft.

4. When the chicken is done, skim the fat off the top of the broth.

5. Take one cup of the chicken broth that has just been cooked and add it to the veggie pot.

6. Blend the veggies and chicken broth together.

7. Shred the chicken pieces and make sure all bones are removed. Add the chicken to the pot of veggies.

Recipe Tips

Here is an old-fashioned homemade dog food recipe. Tastes great, is fast, and is cheap. Additionally, it provides important nutrients to your French Bulldog. Small portions should be given, and the remaining soup should be kept in the fridge. In addition to freezing, you can use it later by putting it in small containers.

Frenchie Meat Loaf

Fall and winter are the seasons for comfort food, and we know our dogs will love to munch on something wholesome and hearty during those months. Our Frenchie family loves this meatloaf recipe because it is creative and looks beautiful. (well, let's be honest, it's the taste). Why not prepare this as a treat for your special furbabies.

SUPER EASY **OVEN BAKE** **COOKED FOOD DIET**

Ingredients

- 1 lbs / 450g. lean ground beef
- 1 ½ cups grated mixed vegetables, use your French Bulldogs favorite vegetables.
- 3 eggs
- ½ cup cottage cheese
- 1 ¾ cups rolled oats

Directions

1. Preheat oven to 350 degrees F. / 175 degrees C.

2. In a bowl, combine all ingredients by hand until well mixed. Make sure the mixture is evenly distributed in the loaf pan.

3. Bake for 40 minutes.

4. Refrigerate or freeze for easy serving.

Recipe Tips

Allow to cool before feeding to your Frenchie. Put the remaining meat loaf into a freezer-friendly container and store them for next time.

Simple Plus Meal

RELATIVELY EASY | **STOVE TOP** | **COOKED FOOD DIET**

Ingredients

- 1 ½ cups brown rice
- 3 carrots, shredded
- 1 tablespoon olive oil
- 2 zucchini, shredded
- 3 pounds ground turkey or chicken
- ½ cup peas, canned or frozen
- 2 ½ cups spinach, chopped
- 3 cups water

Directions

1. In a large saucepan, add the 3 cups of water, add the rice and cook rice according to package instructions, set aside.

2. In a large stockpot or Dutch oven, heat the olive oil over medium heat. Then add the ground turkey or chicken and cook for 3 to 5 minutes.

3. Spinach, carrots, zucchini, peas, and brown rice are added to the pot and stirred for 3-5 minutes until the spinach wilts and the mixture is heated through.

4. Let cool completely before serving to your Frenchie.

Simple Plus Meal

This meal is called Simple Plus because it comprises ingredients you're likely to find in many homemade dog meals – brown rice, chicken or turkey, and veggies. Besides being healthy, it's easy and inexpensive to prepare. This is also a great meal to prepare in bulk, and freeze as single servings.

The Naked Pot Luck Meal!

A raw food diet closely matches the diet that your Frenchies ancestors would also have consumed. It promotes natural ingredients and a combination of vitamins and minerals to provide everything your French Bulldog would want from their food.

The ingredients stay in their raw form because dog food will lose enzymes and nutrients through the cooking process. Also, the recipe avoids the additives that can be present in non-raw foods.

Directions

1. Chop the meat into manageable bite-size pieces.

2. Either blend or par-cook plant ingredients.

3. Add all the ingredients together and mix through.

4. Work out what your French dog needs are for each day and store 3 days' worth in each tub (so you're not taking them out every day).

5. Keep one tub of the mix in the fridge and freeze the rest.

6. Simple! Now watch you happy Frenchie eat.

This recipe

This recipe will produce around 20lbs/10kg of healthy raw Frenchie Bulldog food, which will fit easily in your freezer storage.

Little French Dog

FoR the LOVE of Paws

The Naked Pot Luck Meal!

SLIGHTLY CHALLENGING   **QUICK COOK**   **RAW FOOD DIET**

Ingredients

16.5 lbs/ 7.5kg of Meat & Bone:

- 13 lbs/ 6kg fresh poultry on the bone (e.g. chicken legs or thighs, back or simply in mince with bone form from a provider)
- 2 lbs/ 1kg beef tripe
- 2 lbs/ 1kg raw, whole sardines or oily fish like Mullet
- 2 teaspoons salt
- 1 lb/ 500g beef or sheep hearts
- 1 lb/ 500g beef or sheep livers
- 1lbs/500g beef kidney or sheep

2 lbs/ 1kg of blended plant ingredients:

- 600 lbs/ 300g broccoli
- 600 lbs/ 300g Collard Greens
- 450 lbs/ 200g of carrot
- 450 lbs/ 200g of blueberries/ blackberries

Extras:

- 1 tablespoon of ground pumpkin seed
- 3-5 raw eggs

Beef & Veggie Crockpot

If you own a slow cooker or pressure cooker, this recipe is the ideal candidate for you. You can easily put all the ingredients together and dump them in the cooker. Let it cook before you go to work and come home to find 10-days of homemade French Bulldog food. You can also customize the veggies to the likes of your Frenchie.

SUPER EASY **SLOW COOKER** **COOKED FOOD DIET**

Directions

1. Stir together the beef, corn, carrots, beans, squash, rice, peas and 4 cups water into the slow cooker.

2. Cover the pot with its lid and cook on low heat for 6 hours or high heat for 3 hours.

3. Let it cool before feeding to you French Bulldog.

Ingredients

- 1 ½ cups brown rice
- 1 can kidney beans (425-grams)
- 2.2 lbs/ 1kg ground beef
- 1 ½ cups chopped butternut squash
- 1 ½ cups chopped carrots
- ½ cup peas
- ½ Corn Kernels
- 4 cups of water

Recipe Tips

Allow to cool before feeding to your Frenchie. Put the remaining food into an airtight container and store in fridge.

Salmon Cakes for Dogs with a Dill and Yogurt

SLIGHTLY CHALLENGING

OVEN BAKE

COOKED FOOD DIET

Ingredients

- 14.75 oz/ 500g of canned salmon
- 2 egg whites
- ¼ cup sour cream, low or fat-free
- 2 tsp. dried parsley
- ½ cup carrot, shredded
- ½ cup plain bread crumbs
- 1 tsp. dried dill weed

Yogurt Tartar Sauce:

- ¼ cup plain yogurt, low or fat-free
- ½ tsp. dried dill weed

Directions

1. Preheat oven to 375° F / 190 ° C

2. You will need a baking pan. Place a sheet of baking paper onto the baking pan.

3. Drain the salmon liquid off, make sure to do this very well. (The mixture will be to watery and will not hold together, if not drain well) Skin and bones needs to be removed, if there's any.

4. Mix the plain bread crumbs and the dill in a shallow bowl.

5. Mix salmon, egg whites, sour cream, dried parsley and shredded carrot in a separate medium-sized dish.

6. Scoop a ball shape of salmon mix and gently flatten it into a patty shape.

7. Then thoroughly coat the patty in the breadcrumb mix.

8. Place on to baking pan, spacing them evenly.

10. Bake for approx. 12 minutes. Then flip and bake for 12 more minutes.

11. Cool completely on a wire rack before adding tartar sauce.

Yogurt Tartar Sauce

11. Mix together yogurt and dried dill weed.

12. Lightly cover salmon cakes with sauce and serve.

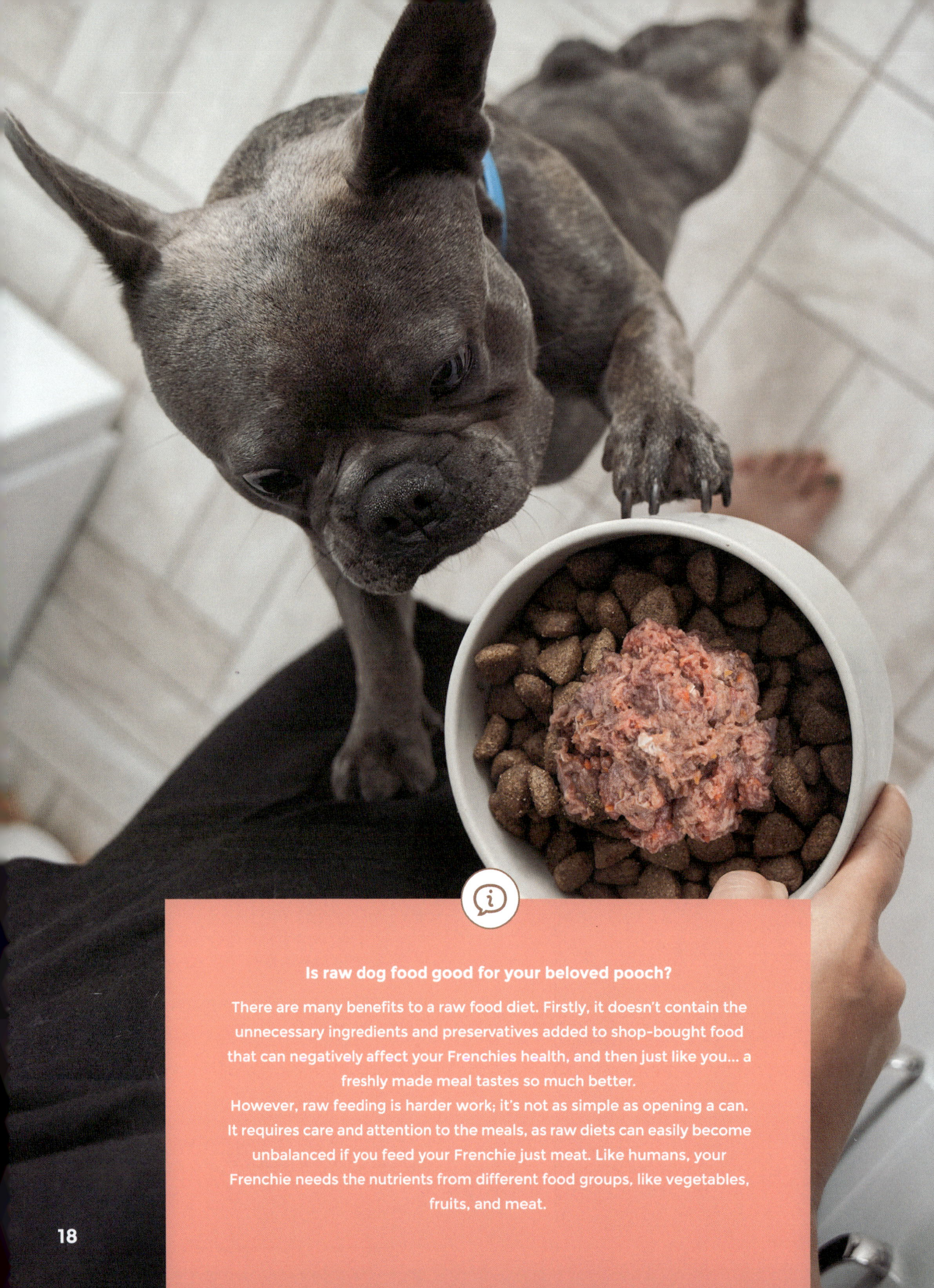

Is raw dog food good for your beloved pooch?

There are many benefits to a raw food diet. Firstly, it doesn't contain the unnecessary ingredients and preservatives added to shop-bought food that can negatively affect your Frenchies health, and then just like you... a freshly made meal tastes so much better.
However, raw feeding is harder work; it's not as simple as opening a can. It requires care and attention to the meals, as raw diets can easily become unbalanced if you feed your Frenchie just meat. Like humans, your Frenchie needs the nutrients from different food groups, like vegetables, fruits, and meat.

The Frenchie Raw Diet Recipe.

The following will make around 22 lbs / 10 kg of raw dog food, that will fit in one small freezer drawer.

What You Will Need Beforehand:

1. A very large bowl or tub for mixing the ingredients together.

2. Depending on your Frenshie's dietery needs, and portion control needs, you would need enough freezer friendly containers for 22 lbs / 10 kg of raw dog food to be stored. You can keep three days' worth in each container.

3. Enough Freezer space for containers.

Directions

1. Chop the meat and organ meat into pieces.

2. Blend or par-cook plant ingredients.

3. Mix all the ingredients together.

4. Add to freezer friendly containers.

5. Refrigerate one tub of the mix and freeze the rest.

RELATIVELY EASY   NO COOKING REQUIRED   RAW FOOD DIET

Ingredients

- 17.5 lbs/ 8kg of meat & bone:
- 12.5 lbs/ 5.5kg / fresh poultry
- 2.2 lbs/ 1 kg raw, whole sardines (frozen). You can also substitute with a few tins of sardines.
- 1 lb/ 500g beef heart
- 1 lb/ 500g beef liver
- 1 lb / 500g beef kidney
- .5 lbs/ 300g broccoli
- .5 lbs/ 300g kale
- .5 lbs/ 300g of carrot
- .5 lbs/ 300g of blueberries or blackberries
- 3-4 raw eggs

Sensitive Stomach Frenchie Recipes

Food Allergies

Food allergies are the most common cause of sensitive stomachs in Frenchies. Similarly to environmental allergies, food allergies can also cause your Frenchies food to not digest properly.

These are simple recipes, but that is what they are meant to be. Its main purpose is to be gentle on their stomachs while still giving them all the nutrients they need.

Chicken Sensitive Stomach Recipe

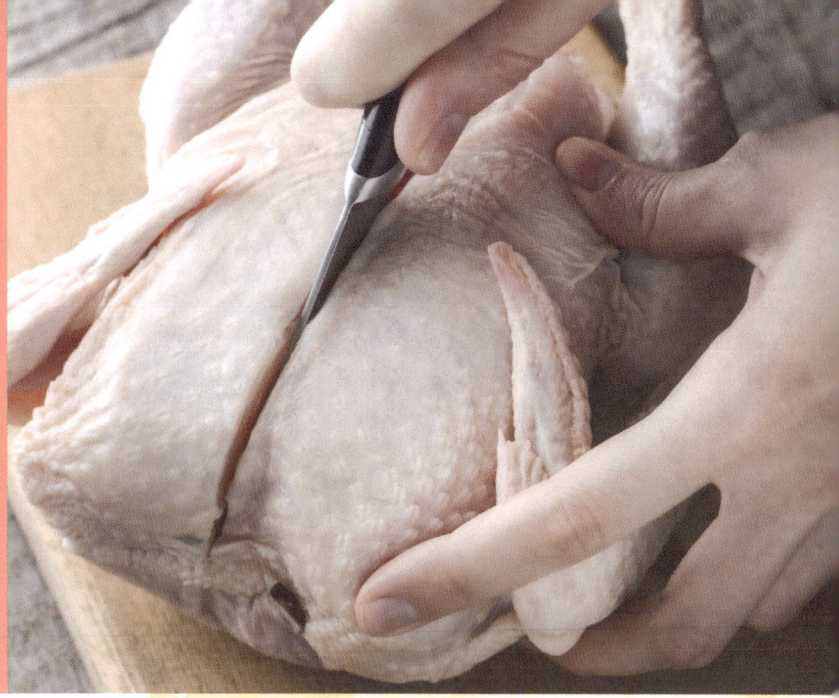

SUPER EASY

STOVE TOP

COOKED FOOD DIET

Ingredients

- 2 cups of white rice
- 1 ½ pound of chopped chicken meat
- 1 ½ cups of carrots and peas vegetable mix.
- 4 ½ cups of water

Directions

1. Add rice, meat, vegetables, and water to a large skillet after heated. Using medium heat, bring the mixture to a boil. You need to simmer all the ingredients, especially white rice, for about 15 minutes after covering the skillet.

2. Both chicken and rice soothe sensitive tummies, so this is an excellent recipe for Frenchies with fragile stomachs.

Recipe Tips

Allow to cool before feeding to your Frenchie. Put the remaining food into an airtight container and store in fridge.

Sensitive Stomach Pumpkin & Chicken Pot

Just because your Frenchie has a sensitive stomach does not mean they cannot have some variety during the week. Here is another recipe that will help keep their stomach soothed and healthy. Depending on your furbabies dietary needs, this recipe will make a few portions, simply package in freezer friendly containers and freeze until their next meal.

RELATIVELY EASY   **STOVE TOP**   **COOKED FOOD DIET**

Directions

1. Begin by placing chicken and vegetables in a large pot.

2. Add water until all ingredients are covered.

3. Once your water begins to boil, lower the heat and leave it on for about 90 minutes or untill chicken and veggies are sorft and tender.

4. Separately, set your rice to cook on the stove or in a rice cooker, whichever you prefer.

5. Beat your eggs and cook until they are firm.

Once chicken and veggies are fully cooked, place in large mixing bowl.

6. Remove the chicken and shred it. Then add shredded chicken back into the mixing bowl with the veggies.

7. Add in the cooked rice, oil, and eggs, one ingredient at a time to the bowl. Stir as you go.

8. This recipe freezes well and is going to last a long time for you and your sensitive Frenchie.

Ingredients

- 2 lbs/ 1 kg of uncooked brown rice
- 2 cans of string beans
- 1 lbs/ 500g of carrots
- 6 eggs
- 6 lbs/ 2.7kg of boneless, skinless chicken breast
- 1 lb / 500g of yams or pumpkin
- ½ cup of sunflower oil

Sensitive Stomach Lamb Pot

To top it off, we have the Lamb and Rice special for your little furball.

SUPER EASY   **STOVE TOP**   **COOKED FOOD DIET**

Directions

1. The lamb must first be prepared. It is best to cube up the lamb to create larger chunks that are chewier. You can also grind it up if you want something simpler.

2. Add oil in a pan and cook the lamb over medium heat. Place a lid on the pan and add just enough water to cover the meat. Let it boil for a few minutes. Simmer the meat by lowering the heat and keeping it covered. Let it simmer for about 30 minutes before draining any excess liquid.

3. While you are doing this, you should cook the brown rice separately. Follow the instructions on the rice box for cooking. Rice usually has to be boiled with about 3 cups of water before it fluffs up.

4. Make sure the rice and meat mixture cools completely. All of the ingredients must be at room temperature before they are combined. It's time to serve the food!

Ingredients

- 7 oz/ 200g of lamb meat
- 1 ½ cups of brown rice
- 1 teaspoon of sunflower oil

SENSITIVE STOMACH RECIPE

Recipe Tips

Vegetables can be a tasty treat to add to this recipe. Carrots and pumpkin can add a bit of sweetness and it goes great with lamb! Remeber to cook it first and just simply add it all together.

SENSITIVE STOMACH RECIPE

Hmmm...COTTAGE PIE!

Cottage Pie is a popular family dish for humans, made from ground beef, veggies and other delicious ingredients. With a few tweaks you can make a cottage pie now for you sensitive stomach frenchie.

Sensitive Stomach Homemade Frenchie Cottage Pie

RELATIVELY EASY   **STOVE TOP**   **COOKED FOOD DIET**

Ingredients

- 1 cup of ground beef
- 1 tbsp. of canola oil
- ½ cup of cooked oatmeal
- 2 hard-boiled eggs
- 2 tbsp. of cottage cheese
- 3 tbsp. of finely chopped beans
- 3 tbsp. of finely chopped carrots

Directions

1. Start by frying the ground beef in canola oil in a heavy pan or skillet. Add the carrot and beans and let simmer for 5min. After cooked, let it cool down. Mix cooked oatmeal in.

2. Finely chop hard-boiled eggs and mix with cottage cheese. Mix well.

3. In a shallow dog bowl, add the mince mixture and then add the eggs/cottage cheese mix on top. Voila doggo cottage pie!

Chicken with Rice Yogurt and Pumpkin

RELATIVELY EASY

STOVE TOP

COOKED FOOD DIET

Ingredients

- 1 ½ cups of white rice
- ½ cup of chicken breasts
- ¼ cup of plain yogurt
- ¼ cup of canned pumpkin / or pumpkin purée
- ½ cup of vegetable mix

Directions

1. Follow the package instructions for cooking white rice.

2. Over medium heat, fill a large pot with water, then boil the chicken breasts until cooked.

3. Par-boil your vegetables.

4. To prepare the meal, shred the chicken into pieces and mix it all together in a medium bowl.

Recipe Tips

Simple and easy to digestible food, this recipe is simple and easy to prepare too. In addition to soothing the stomach, yogurt and pumpkin can help make your Frenchie's bowel movements regular and firm up their stools.

Diet Time...

French Bulldogs are more prone to obesity and food allergies. Yes, it's hard to say no to those big, beautiful eyes... but their health is more important.

As you know, your little Frenchie can be a bit of a food lover. Sometimes they take on the shape of a small barrel running through the house. Now is the time to try a recipe to help them shed the unnecessary weight.

Frenchie Weight Loss Chicken Delight Pot

As you know, your little Frenchie can be a bit of a food lover. Sometimes they take on the shape of a small barrel running through the house. Now is the time to try a recipe to help them shed those pounds and get into shape.

RELATIVELY EASY   **STOVE TOP**   **COOKED FOOD DIET**

Ingredients

- 10 oz/ 290g chicken breast (skinless)
- 5 oz/ 145g brown rice
- 1.6 oz/ 46g broccoli
- 1.6 oz/ 46g carrots
- 1.6 oz/ 46g peas
- 2 ½ teaspoons extra virgin olive oil
- 2 tablespoons psyllium powder

Directions

1. Cook rice until tender- follow packet guidelines.

2. Broccoli, carrots, and peas are steamed until they are just tender.

3. You can steam, microwave, or bake the chicken.

4. Chop the chicken and prepare the vegetables

5. Stir cooked rice and chicken with vegetables.

6. 2 ½ teaspoons of extra virgin olive oil should be added.

7. 2 tablespoons of psyllium powder should be added.

Based on your French Bulldogs diet calorie intake, weigh the final product and portions.

Nutrient Analysis:

This recipe provides 1000 kcal and 76 g protein.

Note: Ingredient weights refer to raw weights.

Nutrient Analysis:

Lean protein like tuna can help your frenchie build healthy muscle, It's low in bad fats that can cause obesity and other health problems.

"Something Fishy" Weight Loss Meal

It is crucial to recognize when your Frenchie becomes overweight and to be able to help your pooch maintain a good healthy weight, so that he/she can lead a happy and healthy life.

SUPER EASY   **STEAM COOKED**   **COOKED FOOD DIET**

Directions

1. Vegetables should be steamed until tender.

2. Mix and dice the vegetables.

3. Combine cooked vegetables with tinned tuna. Break up tuna into small pieces.

4. 2 ½ teaspoons of extra virgin olive oil should be added.

5. Add 1 level tablespoon of psyllium powder.

Ingredients

- 20 oz/ 577g canned tuna in water or brine, drained
- 10.2oz/ 288g potato, scrubbed or peeled
- 4.9 oz/ 138g cauliflower
- 4.9 oz/ 138g green beans
- 2 ½ teaspoons extra virgin olive oil
- 1 tablespoon psyllium powder

Easy-peasy..
Weight Loss Meal

Super busy this week? No time for cooking for your Furbabies? Well, we have you covered with this simple straight to the point recipe.

SUPER EASY **STOVE TOP** **COOKED FOOD DIET**

Ingredients

- One part ground lean meat (chicken, beef, or turkey)
- Three parts pureed pumpkin, cooked carrots, or cooked cabbage
- One part peas or fat-free beans
- ½ cup brown rice bran or ½ cup oats

Directions

1. You only need to lightly brown the meat

2. Add the remaining ingredients and stir until mixed. There you have it! Super simple and easy.

Recipe Tips

You can determine how much chicken is needed to add to a recipe that calls for a measured amount by following the established rule of thumb of one pound of boneless chicken equals about 3 cups of cubed chicken.

The Frenchie Chicken Casserole

On those cold nights where you do not want to take your French Bulldog out for a walk to help them lose weight, but you want something warm, you both can share and help them reduce their calories! Then why not try the Frenchie Chicken Casserole.

SUPER EASY **OVEN BAKE** **COOKED FOOD DIET**

Ingredients

- 3 sliced chicken breasts, cut into bite-size pieces
- 1 ½ cup brown rice
- Approximately 1 cup of steamed carrots and peas
- Cut up 1 celery stalk into small pieces
- 1 cup pumpkin puree (Canned or make your own)
- 2 potatoes
- 4 tbsp unsalted chicken broth

Directions

1. Preheat oven to 300°F/ 150°C

2. Place the chicken and potatoes in a medium-sized saucepan and cover with water. Bring water to boil, then simmer for 30 minutes or untill potatoes are soft and chicken cooked. Drain water and put it aside to cool. After cooled down chop up into bit size pieces.

4. Cook rice separately as per packet instructions.

6. In a large bowl, combine all ingredients. Make sure all the ingrendients was shopped up fist.

Transfer ingredients to a large oven safe bowl or casserole dish without a lid and bake for 20 minutes.

7. Before serving, the chicken casserole should be completely cooled down first.

Recipe Tips

Just like us, our fur-friends enjoy a delicious winter-warmer meal. This is an easy recipe that is warm, hearty and healthy.

Fancy Frenchie Fish Cakes!

RELATIVELY EASY   **STOVE TOP**   **COOKED FOOD DIET**

Ingredients

- Peel and chop 2 large potatoes
- 1 large can of tuna
- 2 cans salmon or tuna
- 4 oz/ 110g frozen peas
- Chopped up hard-boiled eggs, 3 large ones
- Chopped parsley, a large handful will do

Directions

1. Boil potatoes until they are tender. Mash the potatoes thoroughly after they have cooled. ¼ of the parsley should be added.

2. Follow the instructions on the packaging to cook the peas.

3. The salmon, tuna, peas, boiled eggs, and parsley should be mixed together.

4. It is possible to form patties out of the fish mixture according to the size of your French Bulldog and add the potato mixture on top.

5. The potato mixture can also be used to form patties with the salmon and tuna mixed together if you like.

6. Mixture can be kept in the fridge for up to three days if there is any left over.

Recipe Tips
Roll into smaller balls and then freeze for next time.

Just because...

..they are on a diet does not mean your French Bulldog cannot have something fancy now and then. Why not treat them with these wonderful Fancy Frenchie Fish Cakes.

Special Occasions

Your furbaby is loved more than words can tell, and in return, is a loving companion. So, you would take every opportunity to spoil them with treats. It's important not to over-feed with treats. Your pooch still needs to consume plenty of food at mealtimes. While natural dog treats contain essential nutrients, your Frenchie should consume food for its primary nutrition.

Pumpkin Dog Cake

*Makes great Birthday Cakes.
Or bake simply as a treat.*

SLIGHTLY CHALLENGING **OVEN BAKE** **FRENCHIE TREATS**

Ingredients

- 1 ½ cups all-purpose flour, wheat or oat flour may be used as well
- 1 teaspoon baking soda
- ½ teaspoon baking powder
- ¼ teaspoon salt
- ½ teaspoon cinnamon optional
- ¼ cup pumpkin pureé
- ½ cup unsweetened applesauce
- ¼ cup smooth natural peanut butter
- 2 large eggs
- 1-2 tablespoons honey

Peanut Butter Yogurt Frosting:

- 1 cup unsweetened greek yogurt
- ½ cup smooth natural peanut butter
- A tablespoon or two of honey or maple syrup
- 4 dog biscuits for decoration

Directions

1. Preheat oven to 350°F/ 175°C. Grease and flour two 6-inch round baking pans. Set aside.

2. Mix flour, baking soda, baking powder, salt, and cinnamon together in a medium bowl.

3. Beat the pumpkin, applesauce, peanut butter, eggs, and honey together in a bowl with a stand mixer (or with a hand mixer). Add the flour ingredients slowly to the mixer on low and mix just until combined.

4. Then divide the batter equally between the two pans and bake for 30-40 minutes. Cakes should be cooled in pans for about 10 minutes, then inverted onto a wire rack to cool completely.

Peanut Butter Yogurt Frosting:

5. Beat the yogurt, peanut butter and honey with a stand mixer (or a hand mixer) until fluffy and smooth. Your loving Frenchie will love it when you decorate with dog biscuits! Spread the frosting with an offset spatula.

Recipe Tips

Cover the cake with plastic wrap and store it in the refrigerator for up to 4 days.

Note: Consult your Frenchie's veterinarian regarding possible allergies your French dog could have.

Birthday Party Tip:

A party is not a party without some kind of party bag of party treats to take home for your Frenchies fur-friends. Brightly coloured paper bags or noodle boxes with paw prints from your Frenchie.

Fill them with tasty dog treats, both big and tiny. Attach a ball or dog-safe toy, but don't forget your thank you card for joining the party.

NO CHOCOLATE!

Chocolate is a big part of Easter... but do not give it to your Frenchie!

Do not let your French Bulldog eat chocolate. Theobromine in chocolate is highly toxic for dogs. It builds up to dangerous levels in dogs because they are unable to metabolise theobromine efficiently. Chocolate can even lead to death if dogs eat it in excess.

The Frosty Frenchie Easter Treat

These Frenchie favorite frozen snacks, almost too beautiful to eat, yogurt and berries are packed into every bite. Did we note that they are highly nutritious for yourself also? If you are in a warmer climate over Easter, your Frenchie will love you.

SUPER EASY   NO COOKING   FRENCHIE TREATS

Ingredients

- Plain yogurt
- 1 banana
- ½ punnet blueberries
- ½ punnet raspberries
- ½ punnet strawberries.

Directions

1. Blend the fruit in a blender until smooth.

2. Fill a silicone mould halfway with the mixture.

3. Place in the freezer for 60 minutes.

4. Add plain yogurt until it reaches the top of the frozen fruit mix in the mould.

5. Freeze for 2 hours.

Gingerbread Cookies for Frenchies

It is often advised not to give pets gingerbread. Many gingerbread recipes contain nutmeg, which can be toxic for dogs if consumed in excess. There is no nutmeg in this recipe and only Frenchie-friendly ingredients. Still, you should always consult your veterinarian if you have concerns about what you are giving your French Bulldog!

SLIGHTLY CHALLENGING   **OVEN BAKE**   **FRENCHIE TREATS**

Ingredients

- Whole wheat flour, 1 cup
- A cup of rolled oats flour
- A teaspoon of baking powder
- 1 tablespoon of ground ginger
- 1 tablespoon of turmeric
- 1 tablespoon of ground cinnamon
- 2 pinches of ground cloves
- 1/2 teaspoon of allspice
- ¼ cup molasses
- ¾ cup applesauce
- 1 egg
- 1 tsp vanilla extract
- 1 tbsp coconut oil

Directions

1. Preheat oven to 350°F/ 180°C

2. Add the flour, baking powder, and spices to a bowl and mix thoroughly.

3. Mix the molasses and applesauce together until smooth.

4. If more flour is needed, add it along with the egg, vanilla, and coconut oil.

5. Roll gingerbread out and cut into desired sized gingerbread men.

6. If you prefer a soft cookie, bake at 350F / 180C for 20 minutes or until just beginning to brown around the edges. If you prefer a crunchy cookie, bake until the edges are golden brown.

Health Tips

Sugar is required by dogs in the form of carbohydrates, just like humans, but you shouldn't feed your dog granulated sugar or sweets.

Additionally to sugar, dogs shouldn't be given two other types of sweets. If you arent familiar with the effects of xylitol and chocolate, you should read the ingredient labels closely. It is important to keep both of these products far from your Frenchie.

Health Tips

What is the reason dogs cannot eat cooked bones? Whether baked, boiled, steamed, fried or smoked, cooked bones, including leftover bone scraps from your plate, can be dangerous for our pets. During cooking, the collagen and nutrients in bones are leached out, resulting in brittle bones that were previously somewhat flexible and soft. It is easy for a cooked bone to splinter into sharp pieces if it is chewed by an eager Frenchie. In addition to presenting a choking hazard, these jagged splinters can also cause severe internal damage if swallowed

Frenchie Thanksgiving

There are few better special treats for a French Bulldog than homemade turkey dinners. As you prepare your Thanksgiving feast, consider making this homemade dog meal with leftover turkey.

SLIGHTLY CHALLENGING **OVEN BAKE** **COOKED FOOD DIET**

Directions

1. Preheat oven to 350°F/180°C. Lightly oil a roasting pan.

2. Breasts and thighs should be cooked boneless for 30 to 45 minutes; if they are boned, they should be cooked for 45 to 60 minutes, and a whole turkey should be cooked for 1 to 2 hours until the meat juices run clear after piercing them. You need to wait until it cools down.

3. The meat should be diced into large pieces after all the bones have been removed.

4. Sweet potatoes and turkey should be roasted together for about 25-30 minutes until tender. Let cool after peeling, dicing, and slicing.

5. During this time, prepare the oatmeal according to package instructions.

6. Combine the turkey meat, oats, sweet potatoes, and cranberry sauce in a bowl. At this point, you can add gravy or oil and mix thoroughly.

Ingredients

- 3 lb/ 1.3kg skinless turkey pieces
- 1 cup 6 oz/ 175g oatmeal (cooked)
- 2 tbsp cranberry sauce
- 1 lb/ 450g sweet potatoes, cubed
- 4 tbsp turkey gravy

French Bulldog Treats

Treat Time...

You probably love your furbaby more than words can say, and in return, your Frenchie is a loving companion for life. So, you should take every opportunity to spoil them with treats. It is important not to over-feed with treats tho. Your French Bulldog still needs to consume plenty of food at mealtimes. While natural dog treats contain essential nutrients, your Frenchie should be consuming food from their balanced primary nutrition.

Apple Cranberry French Bulldog Treat

RELATIVELY EASY **OVEN BAKE** **FRENCHIE TREATS**

Ingredients

- 1 cup fresh cranberries
- 1 cup apple Sauce
- 1 teaspoon ground Cinnamon
- 2 cups whole wheat flour
- ¼ cup milk

Directions

1. Line a baking sheet with parchment paper or a silicone baking mat and heat the oven to 350°F/180°C.

2. Apple sauce and cranberries should be pureed in a food processor. Add milk, whole wheat flour, cinnamon.

3. Roll out the dough ¼ inch thick on a heavily floured surface. Cut the cookies with your choice of cookie cutter.

4. Bake for 10-15 minutes on a baking sheet covered with parchment paper, until browned.

5. Cool and refrigerate.

Can French Bulldogs eat fruit?

Most fruits are fine for French Bulldogs. When feeding fruit as a snack, make sure it is in moderation, be cautious and remove the seeds, any cores, and some of the skins. Neither grapes nor raisins should be fed to French Bulldogs since they are toxic to dogs and may result in liver failure.

Homemade Beef Jerky

SLIGHTLY CHALLENGING   **DEHYDRATOR OR OVEN**   **FRENCHIE TREATS**

For 1 pound or ½ Kilogram of Meat.

Ingredients

- 1 cup of unsweetened or sugar-free pineapple juice.
- Make the sauce with ½ cup of low-sodium soy sauce. You can substitute regular soy sauce for this if you cannot find this. Nevertheless, we must be careful not to overdo it with salt.
- 1 teaspoon of fish sauce.
- ½ cup apple cider vinegar.
- Pinch of powdered ginger.

Equipment

You will need the following items:

- We use a dehydrator, but your oven at the lowest setting works perfectly, too.
- Zip-lock bag, glass or ceramic container.
- The meat should be placed on a baking tray or a baking sheet with parchment paper if you intend to use the oven for this.

Directions

1. Make a marinade by mixing the ingredients together. As mentioned, each pound of meat needs one lot of marinade.

2. Prepare your lean meats by separating all noticeable fat and discarding first.

3. If you choose to cut the meat into thin slices, keep in mind that they will dehydrate more quickly. Slicing the meat with the grain will produce a chewier treat, while cutting against the grain produces a less chewy one.

4. Place your meat in the marinade, mixing to ensure that it is evenly coated.

5. Marinate in the refrigerator for 4 to 24 hours. The longer, the stronger the flavor.

6. Preheat your dehydrator to 160F / 71C (if you are using your oven set to 160F / 71C) or your lowest temperature.

7. Remove the meat from the marinade, patting dry with a paper towel.

8. Place the trays in the dehydrator, leaving plenty of room between each tray if you can.

9. Test for doneness at 4 hours for the dehydrator, 3 hours if you're using the oven because the temperature may be higher.

10. At least halfway through, the meat should shrink, darken in color, and be dry all the way through. The meat can flex but should not feel rubbery or puffy.

11. When the meat is completely cooled, store it in an airtight container.

12. The jerky should stay fresh for about a week on your counter or two weeks in the refrigerator. You could use a vacuum sealer if you want it to last for a few months.

This homemade chicken, beef and salmon Jerky is great for your French Bulldog and also yourself. This Jerky snack is a chewy, satisfying Frenchie treat that will leave their huge eyes looking for even more.

With no additional additives, such as lots of salt, sugars or carbs, you will feel good sharing these with your little Frenchie any time. If your Frenchie is allergic to beef, stick to chicken or salmon.

Frenchie Ice cream! Yum!

SUPER EASY   **NO COOKING**   **FRENCHIE TREATS**

Carob Chip
- Ice Cream.

Ingredients

- 2 six-ounce containers of low/non-fat, plain yogurt
- 1/3 cup of carob chips
- 1 tbsp. of honey

Directions

1. Mix all the ingredients in a bowl until well-combined.

2. Pour them into cupcake liners or ice cube trays.

3. Freeze until solid.

Peanut Paste
- Ice Cream.

Ingredients

- 1 ripe banana
- 1 cup of peanut butter
- 2 cups of natural plain yogurt
- 2 tbsp. of honey

Directions

1. Mash the banana and then stir it into the natural yogurt.

2. Warm the cup of peanut butter using a microwave or stove until it's easy to stir.

3. The banana and yogurt mixture, as well as the honey, should be added to the softened peanut butter.

4. Mix all ingredients until well-combined.

5. You can freeze the mixture overnight by pouring it into a nonstick container.

On a hot day, who doesn't enjoy some ice cream?

Icy treats are typically irresistible to your Frenchie. Why not make homemade versions of these frozen treats to keep your Frenchie cool. Because normal ice cream can include harmful chemicals, and doggie ice creams can be expensive.

The Frenchie Oats Dog Treats

SLIGHTLY CHALLENGING   **OVEN MAKE**   **FRENCHIE TREATS**

Ingredients

- 2 Cups Flour (Please make sure that your Frenchie is not allergic to wheat before you use flour.)
- 1 cup rolled oats
- 1 ½ cups Water
- Cup smooth peanut butter
- 1 tbsp honey
- ½ tbsp fish oil

Directions

1. Preheat the oven to 350°F/ 180°C

2. Combine the flour and oats in a large mixing bowl.

3. Add 1 cup only of the water (leaving ½ cup). Blend until smooth.

4. Add in the peanut butter, honey, and fish oil and mix until blended well.

5. Slowly add the remaining ½ Cup of water until the mixture has a thick and dough-like consistency.

6. Lightly flour a cooking surface and then roll the dough onto the cooking surface to create a ¼ inch/ 7mm thick sheet.

7. Create shapes you like using your favorite cookie cutter(s).

8. Put some baking paper on your baking sheet before adding the uncooked biscuits.

9. Bake for approximately 40 minutes, but check around 30 minutes.

Recipe Tips

You should allow the finished biscuits to cool before feeding them to your Frenchie. The remaining biscuits should be placed in an airtight container and stored in a cupboard.

Simple Frenchie Peanut Butter Treat

Cookie cutters in the shape of dog bones make these cookies super cute. If you don't have a cookie-cutter in that shape, you can use any shape you want. One way or another, your French Bulldog won't care.

RELATIVELY EASY **OVEN BAKE** **FRENCHIE TREATS**

Ingredients

- 1 cup peanut butter
- 1 cup skim milk
- 1 tablespoon baking powder
- 2 cups whole-wheat flour, plus more for cutting out the cookies

Directions

1. Preheat the oven to 375°F/ 190°C.

2. In a medium mixing bowl, combine peanut butter and milk. You can more efficiently combine milk if you pour it in slowly.

3. Combine the whole-wheat flour and baking powder in another large mixing bowl.

4. Stir in the dry ingredients after combining the peanut butter and milk. The ingredients should be thoroughly mixed together.

5. On a sheet of parchment paper, sprinkle a little wheat flour and roll the dough out to the desired thicken

6. Bake for 15 to 20 minutes.

Recipe Tips

Peanut butter is easy to cook with because it melts easily, so you can easily incorporate it into recipes.

Frozen Frenchie Watermelon

Keep your Frenchie hydrated this summer with these refreshing watermelon French Bulldog treats. Your furbabies will love to cool down with a few of these wonderful treats.

SUPER EASY   **NO COOKING**   **FRENCHIE TREATS**

Ingredients

- 2 cups seedless watermelon pureed
- ½ cup plain greek yogurt

Directions

1. Blend seedless watermelon in a blender. (You can use a normal watermelon but make sure all seeds are removed)

2. Fill ¼ of the ice tray with yogurt. Let it freeze for 1 hour.

3. Add the watermelon pureed over to top of the yogurt. Make sure to freeze for at least 4 hours or overnight.

4. Keep frozen until ready to serve.

Can your dog eat watermelon?

Yes, watermelon makes a good treat for your dog. With high moisture content and fiber content, along with densely packed nutrients, it belongs to the category of superfoods.

Recipe Tips

Allow cup cakes to cool before feeding to your Frenchie. Put the remaining cup cakes into an airtight container and store in a cupboard.

Carrot Frenchie Cup Cakes

RELATIVELY EASY   OVEN BAKE   FRENCHIE TREATS

Ingredients

- ½ cup buckwheat flour
- 1 teaspoon baking powder
- 1 tablespoon honey
- 1 egg
- ½ cup coconut milk
- ½ cup grated carrot
- ¼ cup coconut oil

Icing

- 50g yogurt drops
- 1 tablespoon coconut oil
- grated carrot

Directions

1. Preheat oven to 320°F/ 160°C

2. Baking powder and honey should be mixed well in a bowl. Stir buckwheat flour, coconut oil, coconut milk, and egg together until well combined. Mix grated carrot through.

3. Divide evenly into cupcake pan, then bake in the oven for 15 20 minutes.

4. Melt yogurt drops and coconut oil over low heat, then drizzle over cooled cupcakes.

5. Grate carrots over cupcakes before the yogurt icing sets.

Can I Give My Dog Pumpkin?

The pumpkin is an excellent food for French Bulldogs. It is loaded with essential micro-nutrients and fiber, which makes it a very nutritious snack. Pumpkin is beneficial for dogs not only as a natural stomach soother, but also for removing excess water from their intestines.

Non-Bake Pumpkin and Oat Treats Dinner

These no-bake pumpkin and oat treats are a great option for anyone looking for an easy homemade French Bulldog treat recipe that doesn't require them to be baked. Aside from being delicious and full of fall flavors, they are also loaded with fiber, vitamins, and minerals.

SUPER EASY   **NO COOKING**   **FRENCHIE TREATS**

Ingredients

- 2 ½ cups (350g) old-fashioned oats
- ¾ cups (170 g) canned pumpkin puree
- ¼ cup (60ml) warm water

Directions

1. Combine the pumpkin and water in a mixing bowl, stirring until well combined.

2. Add the oats and stir until the mixture starts to come together.

3. Pinch off pieces of dough and roll them into small balls by hand then place them on a parchment-lined plate.

4. Roll the balls in extra oats, if desired, then chill for 24 hours until firm.

Frenchie Smoothie's

These smoothies contain vitamins, antioxidants, and protein in abundance. Additionally, parsley will help eliminate bad breath your French Bulldog may be suffering from.

SUPER EASY   **BLENDER**   **FRENCHIE TREATS**

Ingredients

- 2/3 cup almond milk
- 1 cup chopped carrots
- ½ cup greek yogurt (plain)
- ¼ cup fresh parsley

Directions

1. Combine all ingredients in a blender.
2. Blend until smooth.

Is Yogurt Good For Dogs?

Yes, it is! It's best to buy plain yogurt or non-fat plain yogurt. Just make sure there are no artificial preservatives or sweeteners in the yogurt.

Cheesy Doggo Biscuit Recipe

SLIGHTLY CHALLENGING **OVEN BAKE** **FRENCHIE TREATS**

Ingredients

- 2 ½ cups whole wheat flour
- 2/3 cup parmesan cheese, grated
- 2 cups cheddar cheese, grated
- ¼ cup extra virgin olive oil
- 2 eggs, lightly beaten
- ½ cup unsweetened applesauce

Cheese & Peanut Butter Filling:

- ½ cup peanut butter, creamy or chunky
- 8 ounces/ 220 grams of cream cheese, fat-free

Directions

1. Preheat oven to 400°F/ 205°C

2. In a large bowl, combine the flour, cheddar, and parmesan cheese.

3. Whisk together the two eggs in a small bowl.

4. Applesauce and extra virgin olive oil should be stirred together.

5. Make a well in the dry ingredients.

6. Add the applesauce to the dry ingredients and stir until the dough comes together.

7. Cooking spray should be lightly sprayed on a baking sheet.

8. Then, fill the scoop with the cheesy mixture using a tablespoon-sized cookie scooper.

9. Put the scoops on the baking sheet close together, since they don't rise in the oven.

10. Cook for 20 minutes. Once the oven has been turned off, let the dog treats cool in there.

It is best to flatten the rounded cookie if you are making cheese sandwiches with cheese dip.

Filling:

1. In a microwaveable dish, combine cream cheese and peanut butter.

2. Microwave the ingredients for 10 seconds at a time, stirring each time until the mixture is easily combined.

3. Use a butter knife to spread the filling

4. It is also possible to place the cheese mixture in a zip-top bag and seal it. The mixture can be squeezed out like icing from the bottle after cutting off the tip.

FRENCHIES LOVES THEIR TREATS!

Baking fresh homemade dog Biscuits for your French Bulldog will let them know you care about them! (of course) The Cheddar Dog Biscuits are made for Frenchie, who loves cheese.

Can your dog eat pears?

Pears are packed with copper, vitamins C and K, and fiber, making them excellent treats. Several studies suggest that eating pears reduces the chance of having a stroke by half. Remove the seeds from pears by cutting the fruit into bite-size chunks first and removing the pit. If canned pears contain sugary syrups, don't buy them for you Frenchie.

Frenchie Pear, and natural yogurt smoothie

Your French Bulldog will love this smoothie. Fruits like pears are hydrating and low in calories. In addition to their high fiber and potassium content, they promote better intestinal movement and prevent cardiovascular diseases. In addition to its protein content, yogurt with reduced sugar has important anti-inflammatory and antioxidant properties.

SUPER EASY   **BLENDER**   **FRENCHIE TREATS**

Ingredients

- 1 pear
- Half a cup of natural sugar-free yogurt
- 1 teaspoon of ground cinnamon

Directions

1. Cut the pear into medium-sized pieces after washing it and make sure you have removed all the seeds.

2. Next, you need to blend all of the ingredients to create the perfect smoothie for your Frenchie.

Frenchie Frozen Applesauce Treat

On those hot summer days, your French Bulldog is going to love you when you offer them one of these frozen applesauce treats.

SUPER EASY   **BLENDER**   **FRENCHIE TREATS**

Ingredients

- 1 cup of non-sweetened applesauce
- 1 Royal Gala Apple (or Similar)
- 1 cup of plain yogurt
- 1 ½ tablespoons of Brewer's yeast
- ½ teaspoon cinnamon

Directions

1. The yogurt, applesauce, Brewer's yeast, and cinnamon should be blended together. Combine all ingredients in a blender and blend for 1 minute. The mixture should be smooth so that it can be poured easily.

2. Chop the Apple up in small chunks and add to mixture.

2. You should then pour the contents into silicone mold or ice cube trays.

3. Put the ice trays in the freezer and leave them there overnight for them to solidify.

4. Your French Bulldog can eat the treats as soon as they are taken out. They'll love it!

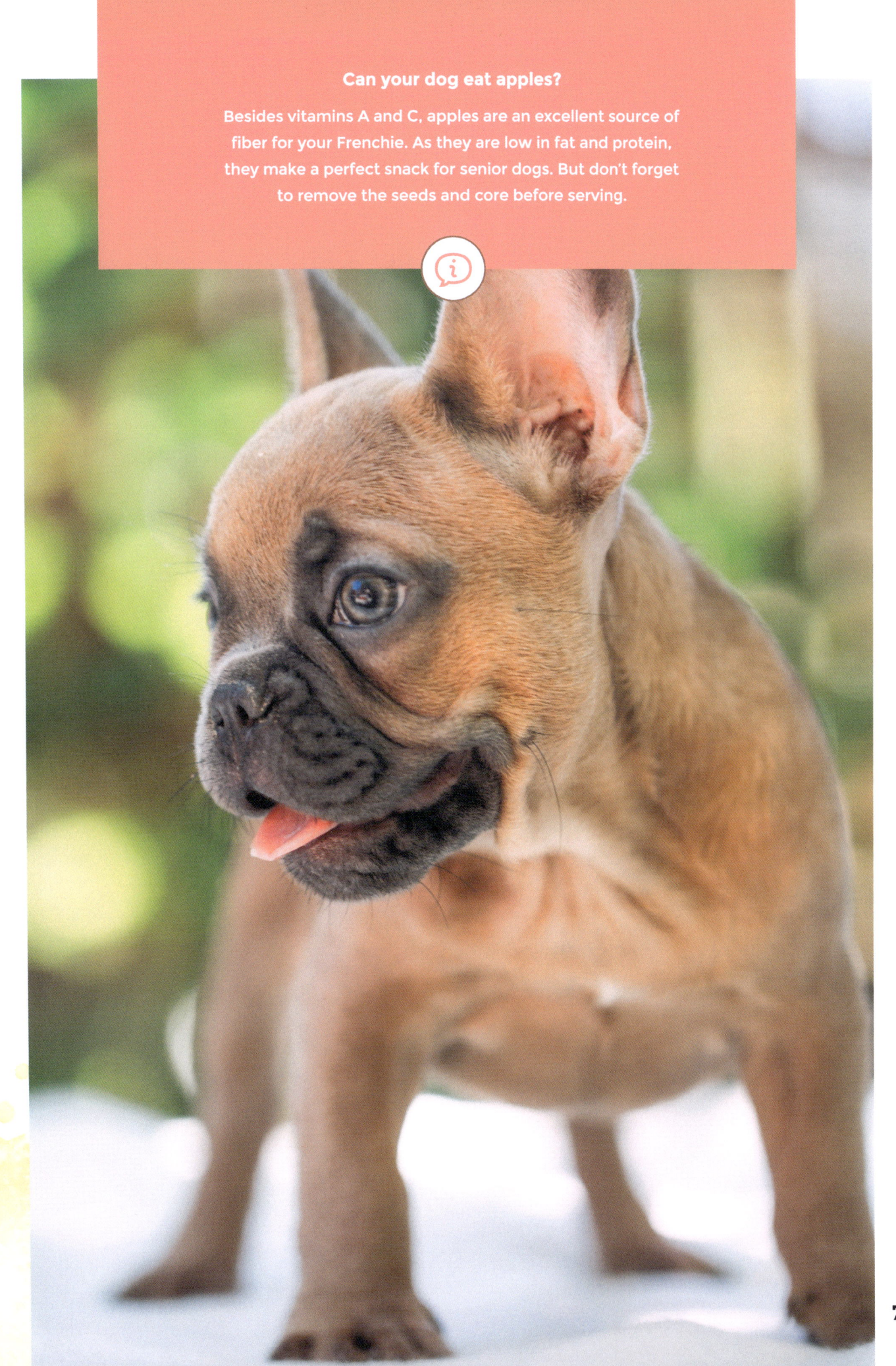

Can your dog eat apples?

Besides vitamins A and C, apples are an excellent source of fiber for your Frenchie. As they are low in fat and protein, they make a perfect snack for senior dogs. But don't forget to remove the seeds and core before serving.

Printed in Great Britain
by Amazon